TopGear

BEST BITS

Winter Olympics

VRRROOOMMM

TopGe

BBC Children's Books
Published by the Penguin Group
Penguin Books Ltd, 80 Strand, London WC2R 0RL, England
Penguin Group (Australia) Ltd, 250 Camberwell Road,
Camberwell, Victoria 3124, Australia (a division of Pearson
Australia Group Pty Ltd)
Canada, India, New Zealand, South Africa

Published by BBC Children's Books, 2008
Text and design © Children's Character Books, 2008

10 9 8 7 6 5 4 3 2 1

Written by Jonathan Empson
Designed by Dan Newman

ISBN: 978-1 40590-460-5

Printed in China

I **don't** want to
eat **yellow snow!**

Contents

I don't want to **die** in **tights!**

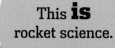

This **is** rocket science.

Introduction

> **Welcome** to the Top Gear Winter Olympics!

Welcome to the Top Gear Winter Olympics! The official Winter Olympics are OK, but they're a bit, well, quiet. Sure, the skiers and skaters do a lot of swooshing and heavy breathing, but we want screaming engines, squealing tyres and grinding metal.

So we've come to Norway to rev things up a bit. We thought it would be fun to do a biathlon in a 4x4, to send a Mini down a ski jump, and to play a violent game of ice hockey with ten small hatchbacks. And for style points, we decided to try ice dancing in a Jaguar.

Like the real Olympics, these Top Gear events are open to any entrant regardless of nationality: our car contestants are from Britain, Germany, Japan, Sweden and... um, actually, that's about it.

To steer these cars to victory, we've chosen some expert drivers – or, failing that, Top Gear presenters. Namely Jeremy Clarkson (the tall, loud one), Richard Hammond (the small, cuddly one) and James May (the medium-sized, slow one). Also making an appearance – in our dramatic finale – is The Stig.

We're confident Olympic organisers will embrace these brilliant new ideas and start building car-size podiums. If they don't, we'll run them over.

Let the games begin!

Faster, Higher, Stronger...Power!

Biathlon

In the Winter Olympics, the biathlon involves a cross-country ski race and hitting targets at a rifle range. The Top Gear biathlon, however, involves racing 4x4s in snow and (probably) missing targets at a rifle range.

Eat **6000** calories a day? That means **I** could be a biathlete!

Interesting biathlon facts

The first biathlon competition took place in 1767, which is also the year James last cut his hair and Jeremy last admitted being wrong about something.

Olympic biathlon events are run over 6km, 7.5km, 10km, 12.5km, 15km or 20km.
(Tip: always check which event you're in before setting out.)

Biathletes in training need to consume 6,000 calories daily – the equivalent of 2lb of butter, 70 slices of bread, 112 eggs, 117 biscuits, 21 Twix bars or half a Richard Hammond.

The plan

01 James and Jeremy will race their cars around a 3km track. Handling, weight, traction and not driving into a tree are very important here.

02 Then they have to hit five targets on a rifle range from a standing position.

03 It's five seconds in the penalty box for each target they miss...

04 ... before they do a second 3km circuit.

05 Then it's another round of shooting, from a lying-down position in the back of their cars. (They'll have to work out how to fold the seats down first.)

06 More penalties (surely not?!).

07 Then a sprint to the finish.

08 The winner gets gold. The loser gets to eat 'golden snow'.

The contenders

All we need for this event are two 4x4s, two drivers and two guns.

Driver 1: James May

Pie enthusiast James is the world's most reluctant Arctic explorer, due to the North Pole's lack of pie shops. In fact, he's not that keen on snow at all, yet he's determined to win this challenge.

Car 1: Audi Q7

Audi let Porsche build an SUV first, then copied it. Sadly, Porsche locked the best off-road bits from its stonking Cayenne in a cupboard and hid the key.

Gun 1: Standard .22 biathlon rifle

James would be more at home in a military band than the infantry, but he's not bad on the trigger – as long as his fringe doesn't fall over the scope.

It's a **full 3%** uglier than a troll.

0-62mph: 9.1secs ***Top speed:*** 169mph ***Power:*** 233bhp

Driver 2: Jeremy Clarkson

Jeremy lives in the English countryside – an area not known for avalanches, reindeer and other snowy things. Yet he still fancies his chances. What a surprise.

Gun 2: Heckler & Koch MP5

This machine pistol fires 800 rounds a minute. Jeremy's hoping at least five of them hit the target.

A **brilliant** car. It's like a faithful old **Labrador.**

0-62mph: 10.9secs **Top speed:** 121mph **Power:** 185bhp

Car 2: Volvo XC90

A cunning choice by Jeremy. First, it's built in neighbouring Sweden, where they know a thing or two about driving on icy roads. Second, he actually owns one, so he knows how they work. Or THINKS he does.

Go!

It's Audi versus Volvo, Captain Slow versus Jezza, as they line up for the start.

James grabs an early lead in the more powerful Audi and manages to get it airborne – lucky he's got his pilot's licence.

Jeremy is so shocked by Captain Slow's speed, he crashes and starts to lose valuable time – James arrives at the rifle range well in front.

I don't want to eat **golden snow!**

Oooh!

BA-DOOM

Five out of five to beat, Volvo man!

James lines up the target. Like a real biathlete, he has to time his shot so his heartbeat and breathing don't upset his aim. Amazingly, he gets a perfect score. He's leaving as Jeremy arrives.

There's a five-second penalty for each miss, putting James a whole minute in front by the time Jeremy gets back on the track. But Jeremy can't catch up and James does a flawless second lap.

BLAM BLAM BLAM

Penalty

Jeremy's turn to shoot. There's no rule about using standard biathlon rifles, so Jeremy's chosen a machine gun... But he manages to miss every single target. Maybe he should have kept his eyes open.

Power!

VRROOOM!

James arrives back at the rifle range, backs his Audi up to the shooting position and drops the rear seats easily. Unfortunately, he ruins his perfect shooting record.

I've missed a couple!

No! He's getting ahead!

But somehow a tree falls down behind the target. Coincidence? Or is Jeremy the first man ever to shoot a tree to death?

Jeremy arrives as James is leaving, and does his best to get in the Audi's way. As James does his time in the penalty box, Jeremy fails to work out how to lower the rear seats.

Another 25 seconds for Jeremy in the penalty box. Surely the race is lost?

But no! James crashes!

He's forced to phone Mrs Clarkson for instructions. When he *finally* gets the seats down, he takes aim. Jeremy maintains his perfect record: five out of five misses.

Jeremy drives his Volvo like no Volvo has ever been driven before. As James frantically digs out his car and gets back on the track – Jeremy appears.

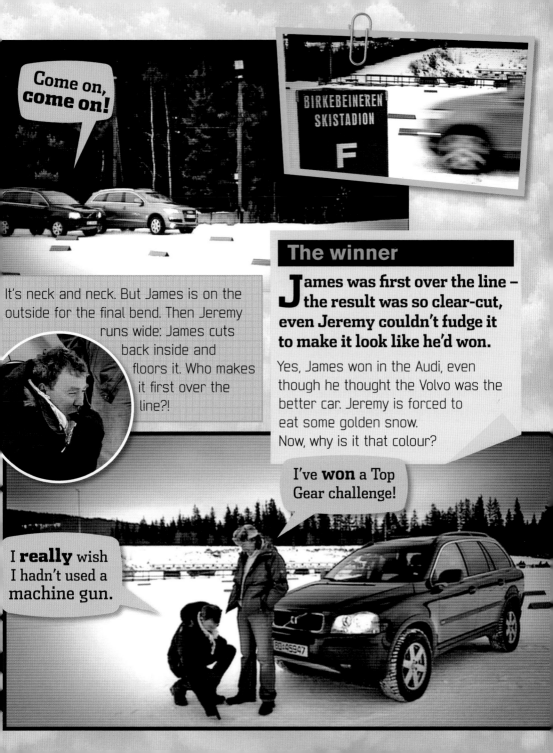

Come on, **come on!**

BIRKEBEINEREN SKISTADION F

It's neck and neck. But James is on the outside for the final bend. Then Jeremy runs wide: James cuts back inside and floors it. Who makes it first over the line?!

The winner

James was first over the line – the result was so clear-cut, even Jeremy couldn't fudge it to make it look like he'd won.

Yes, James won in the Audi, even though he thought the Volvo was the better car. Jeremy is forced to eat some golden snow. Now, why is it that colour?

I've **won** a Top Gear challenge!

I **really** wish I hadn't used a machine gun.

Speed Skating

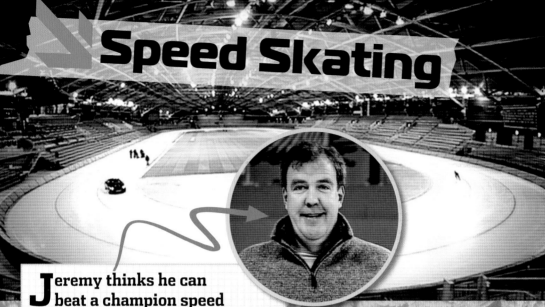

Jeremy thinks he can beat a champion speed skater around an ice rink in a rear-wheel drive Jaguar XK. When most people hear the words 'ice rink', they think 'very slippery' – but not Jeremy, apparently.

The plan

01 Jeremy and Jaguar will set off from the start at the same time as Eskil Ervik, the 1,500m speed skating world record holder, who'll be wearing an outfit much tighter than Jeremy's jeans and more sleek and shiny than James' hair.

02 It's a three-lap, 1,500m race.

03 First over the line wins.

Go!

James fires the starting pistol and Eskil digs in and powers off the line. But Jeremy doesn't. The Jag's wheels spin uselessly on the slick surface.

By the time Jeremy gets on to the back straight, Eskil's already at the end of it as the Jag slides and spins into barriers – luckily they bounce him right back.

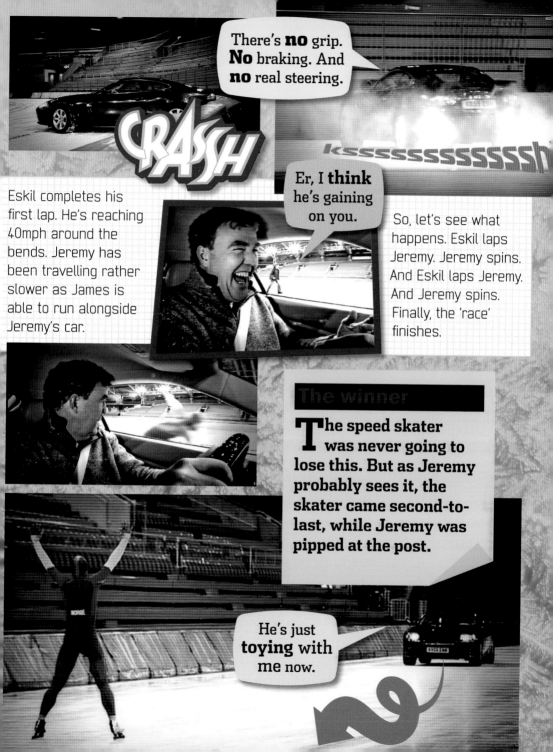

Frozen Lake Race

OK, there's no direct equivalent of this in the Winter Olympics, but Jeremy was keen to discover how the Jaguar XK would be at 'off-road-slalom-speed-dance-skating'. A perfectly sensible question, eh? Well, not really. But Jeremy believes that a light and powerful two-wheel drive car will be faster round a flat ice track than a heavier 4x4.

The plan

01 First, they find a frozen lake – one covered in snow, just for an extra challenge.

02 Jeremy gets a hole drilled in the ice to make sure it's thick enough to take the weight of James' 3 tonne 4x4. He finds it's only a 5in thick. He decides not to worry James with this detail – James thinks it about 5ft thick.

> Do people fall through the ice in frozen lakes?

> There were two last week.

> You'll need four-wheel drive!

> Are they dead?

> You **won't!**

> **Quite** dead.

03 James then designs a track with a stick and some snow.

a. Start line.
b. Long, sweeping curve.
c. Straight.
d. Small sweeping curves.
e. Another long, sweeping curve.
f. Some more small sweeping curves.
g. Then another, ahh, sweeping curve to the finish line.

04 James then creates the track, using a much-more-than-3-tonne tractor, while Jeremy practises.

05 Miraculously, both survive step 4.

06 Race on!

Where Jeremy will **crash** if he hasn't already.

here Jeremy
ll get carried
ay and apply
e '**power!**'

a
b
c
d
e
f
g

It's the best 4x4 of all time (according to the Hamster).

0-62mph: 8.0secs **Top speed:** 121mph **Power:** 295bhp

Car 1: Land Rover Discovery 3

James' choice for a 4x4 is the 'Disco'. It's got a 295bhp, V8 engine – basically the same engine used in the Jaguar. It's also got all kinds of four-wheel drive gadgetry, so even a complete idiot could drive it upside down on a cloud, no problem.

The contenders

This event will be a simple race against the clock. It's only light for about two minutes a day this far north, so James and Jeremy will try to finish before nightfall. And the way Jeremy's been spinning all over the place in practice, that could be a tough challenge.

It goes like a **starship!**

Car 2: Jaguar XK

Only the back wheels are driven in Jeremy's car, and he's hoping they'll work and won't end up facing the wrong way on the track. We'll see. The 300bhp, V8 is made of aluminium, like the car's body, so the low weight means it's very fast and unlikely to suddenly disappear mid-lap to the sound of cracking ice.

0-62mph: 6.0secs   *Top speed:* 155mph   *Power:* 300bhp

Go!

And we're off!

James will be the first to take to the track. If his Land Rover does indeed fall through thin ice, Jeremy will probably claim victory by default.

James is fast off the line thanks to four-wheel drive. Like the man himself, the Disco is very calm and controlled in the first corners.

Thanks to the car's smart traction control, James doesn't even break a sweat. Mind you, it's hard to sweat when it's this cold. Jeremy watches from the sidelines rather unimpressed.

I thought I heard the ice crack.

Nice bit of drift there...

James does a beautiful drift towards the finish line, crossing in 2min 3secs.

Now it's Jeremy's turn and he reveals to James that the ice is only 5in thick, and that he is lucky to be alive.

...Flick it the other way...

You were hardly **moving.**

With that parting comment, Jeremy fishtails off the line, but is soon back in control for the first long bend. But things soon start looking ugly. Jeremy pulls off his first ice-dancing move: a pirouette.

I'm sideways, I'm controlled. I look **good.**

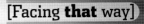
[Facing **that** way]

[Going **that** way]

I **want** one of these lakes. **Power!**

James is unimpressed. Jeremy miraculously manages to start pointing the right way again, and wobbles around the track to the final corner.

In a spectacularly terrible finish, Jeremy slides off into a snow bank, then gets bogged in the snow.

The judges are looking for something **elegant**, something **pretty!**

The race is over. Will Jeremy still try to claim he won? Is snow white?

Oh, no!

CRASSH

22

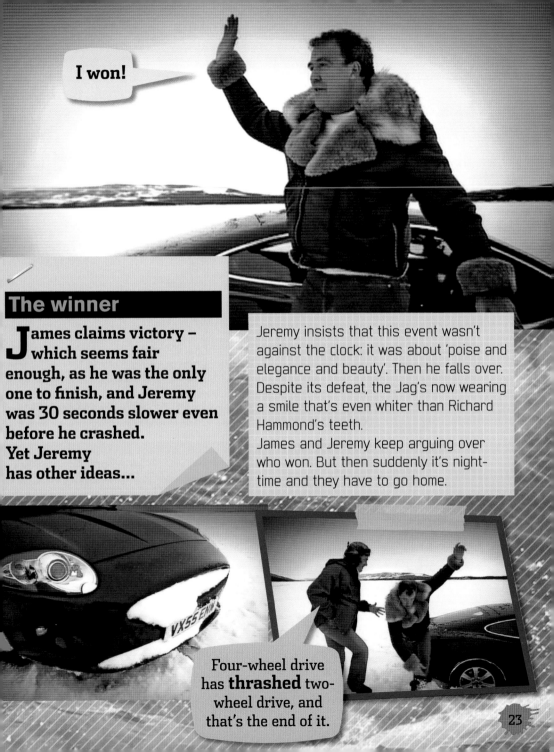

I won!

The winner

James claims victory – which seems fair enough, as he was the only one to finish, and Jeremy was 30 seconds slower even before he crashed. Yet Jeremy has other ideas...

Jeremy insists that this event wasn't against the clock: it was about 'poise and elegance and beauty'. Then he falls over. Despite its defeat, the Jag's now wearing a smile that's even whiter than Richard Hammond's teeth.

James and Jeremy keep arguing over who won. But then suddenly it's night-time and they have to go home.

Four-wheel drive has **thrashed** two-wheel drive, and that's the end of it.

Bobsleigh Run

In this event, a car will race a bobsleigh. Sure, a bobsleigh doesn't even have an engine, but it can still get down the track in less than a minute. (And no, we're not sending the car down the bobsleigh track.)

This is **slippery**, **dangerous** and full of difficult corners.

The plan

01 The four-man crew will push off the bobsleigh at the start line, then jump in.

02 At the same time, the car will set off. It has to drive down a road that finishes at the same place as the bobsleigh track. The road is about the same length as the track – 1,365 metres. (That's 0.848171677 miles. Roughly.)

03 The bobsleigh's relying on gravity – the track descends 114m vertically. The car's relying on acceleration.

04 First team across the line wins!

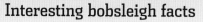

Interesting bobsleigh facts

Bobsleighs can hit 80mph.

Bobsleigh crews are exposed to forces of over 6g on the track – meaning they feel six times heavier.

Like most sports, it was invented by Britons. (They were on holiday in Switzerland at the time.)

Like most sports, it's called something else by the Americans (bobsledding). They also claim they invented it.

The person who steers the bobsleigh is called the pilot (though if it actually leaves the ground, he's done something badly wrong).

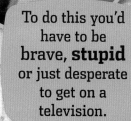

To do this you'd have to be **brave, stupid** or just desperate to get on a television.

01
02
03
04

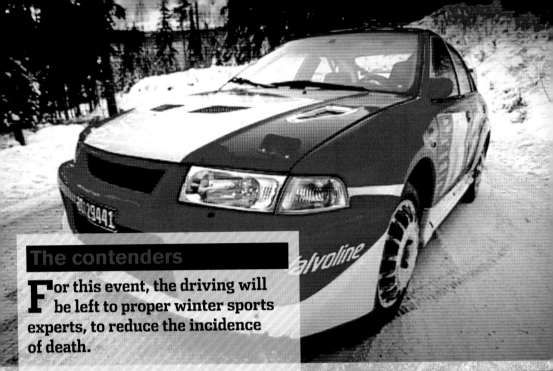

The contenders

For this event, the driving will be left to proper winter sports experts, to reduce the incidence of death.

The Car: Mitsubishi Evo World Rally Car

It has four-wheel drive, a turbocharged 300bhp engine and 420 spikes in each tyre for grip. The driver is Henning Solberg, the Norwegian National Rally Champion. Strapped tightly into the navigator's seat (so he can't run away) is James May. Henning is nervous – until someone tells him James won't actually be navigating.

You're wearing **tights!**

The Bobsleigh: A Bobsleigh

The bob, with its aerodynamic composite body, weighs a maximum of 630kg, including crew. The four-man team consists of three ultra-fit Norwegian Olympic athletes... and Richard Hammond. Richard's worried because the pilot says that, after years of bobsleighing, he's 3cm shorter than he used to be – all because of the g-forces.

Richard in training

James in training

Top speed: *80mph* **Power:** *3g-forces!*

I can't **afford** to lose 3cm!

Go!

The bobsleigh is being timed by the course computer; James is timing the car on a stopwatch. The start is critical here. A second lost by the bobsleigh team at the top of the run will make them three seconds slower at the bottom.

They're off! The bobsleigh team push the bob for almost 50m then jump aboard. The bob hits the first turn and Richard holds his breath, and not just from terror – holding their breath helps support a bobsleigher's body against the g-forces.

Mind the trees, you **nutter!**

James is relaxed (well, sort of) and enjoying watching an expert work the sharp and dangerous turns. And as only Richard can, he looks like he's been shaken about like a – you guessed it – hamster in a cage.

Henning charges on, the bob charges on, and James and Richard both become more and more terrified. At the midpoint, it's neck and neck.

Then there's a mistake: the bob bounces off the side of the track.

If the bob overturns, it will keep sliding right to the bottom of the track – on the head of the tallest passenger. But at least that won't be Richard.

I don't want to **die** in **tights!**

The finish line flashes past and James hits the stopwatch button. Henning stops the car by spinning it. That was probably really necessary.
Both Richard and James can't wait to get out and check the scoreboard and James' stopwatch. Who won?!

ARRRGGH!

I'm **broken!**

The winner

It's the worst possible result for car fans. Unless Captain Slow's messed up the only thing he had to do – press the stopwatch button on time – it seems Henning crossed the line in 1min 2.24secs. The bobsleigh is the winner at 59.68 seconds! James can hardly stand the shame...

We **did** it!

Ice Hockey

Ice hockey in cars. Well, why not? Top Gear's played football with cars before. There was much car damage, but no-one was injured. Ice hockey, however, is a much more violent sport...

*If there's a **death,** you have to put someone in the **sin bin.***

*And **that's** when I blow my horn?*

The plan

01 It's five-a-side, with both teams driving nimble Suzuki Swifts.

02 James May (blue team) and Richard Hammond (red team) are the captains. Their teammates are all local rally drivers.

03 The aim of the game is to get the inflatable puck in the opponent's goal, using the cars to nudge it along.

04 Jeremy Clarkson will attempt to referee, armed with an air horn, a megaphone and some lager. We just know he'll be fair and just, even though he seems unsure of the rules or how to operate the airhorn.

Interesting ice hockey facts

Ice hockey is so violent, it has official rules for fighting in a game.

No one's quite sure who invented ice hockey, but one theory goes that it was British soldiers stationed in Canada. So let's go with that.

A game was played on a frozen lake at Buckingham Palace in 1895.

¡Go!

PAAARRRRRRP

It's time for the face-off (as they call the kick-off in ice hockey). James May faces Richard Hammond across the centre circle. Jeremy blows the horn for the start and inside a minute, Hammond's Reds have scored!
It's 1–0!

James attempts a football-style commentary as he storms towards the goal.
James passes... but it's forced wide and Jeremy starts to show worrying bias. And thanks to his support, James' Blues... miss again.

Goooooaaaaal!

Oh, he's up like a salmon!

Oh come on!

The Reds grab another two quick goals. 3–0. But when the Blues finally get one back, the ref falls over and misses seeing the goal. Fortunately for James, the ref's prepared to take his word for the fact that they did score. Richard is not happy. 3–1.

Jeremy shows even more bias by placing the puck right in front of James' car for the restart. Sure enough, James scores immediately. 3–2.

James then crashes into his own man, leaving the goal wide open for Richard to boot it home. The score? Red: 4. Blues: 2.

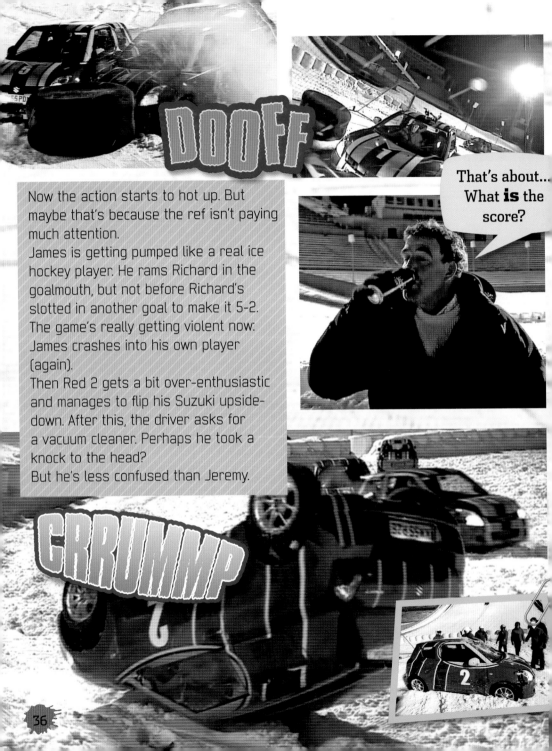

DOOFF

Now the action starts to hot up. But maybe that's because the ref isn't paying much attention.

James is getting pumped like a real ice hockey player. He rams Richard in the goalmouth, but not before Richard's slotted in another goal to make it 5-2.

The game's really getting violent now: James crashes into his own player (again).

Then Red 2 gets a bit over-enthusiastic and manages to flip his Suzuki upside-down. After this, the driver asks for a vacuum cleaner. Perhaps he took a knock to the head?

But he's less confused than Jeremy.

That's about... What **is** the score?

CRRUMMP

In the dying moments of the game, Richard takes out James. The ref acts decisively.

With the Reds a man down, the Blues get another two goals. 5–4! Richard gets back on the ice... just in time for the cackling ref to blow the final horn!

KKRNTCH

Hammond, in the sin bin!

How was the snow?

The winner

To Jeremy's dismay, Richard Hammond chalks up a 5–4 victory. To Jeremy's pleasure, this means he gets to see James eating golden snow for a change.

It was **golden,** thank you.

Ski Jump

Can a rusty Leyland Mini leap further than a man? How about sending them both down a ski jump to find out? We think this might end badly, so no one will be in the Mini at the time.

Interesting ski jump facts

Ski jumping was invented in Norway.

The slopes are angled at around 35–38 degrees. So a good 4x4 could drive up it – as long as its tyres aren't bald.

Ski jumpers usually fly for 100-130 metres – longer than a football pitch.

There's a more extreme form called ski flying – the world record distance is 239m.

The maths is quite simple. It's $v = u + at$.

Let's have a cup of tea.

The plan part I

01 James May does the complex calculations, factoring in gravity, mass, acceleration, trajectory, wind resistance...

02 Jeremy and Richard help by drinking tea and keeping quiet.

03 James discovers that gravity and the Mini's feeble engine will not be enough.

The plan part II

01 James will work out how to steer the car so it leaves the jump head first.

02 Richard will work out how to stop the car so it doesn't take out a small Norwegian town.

03 Jeremy will work out how to make the car go faster.

I'll do the power!

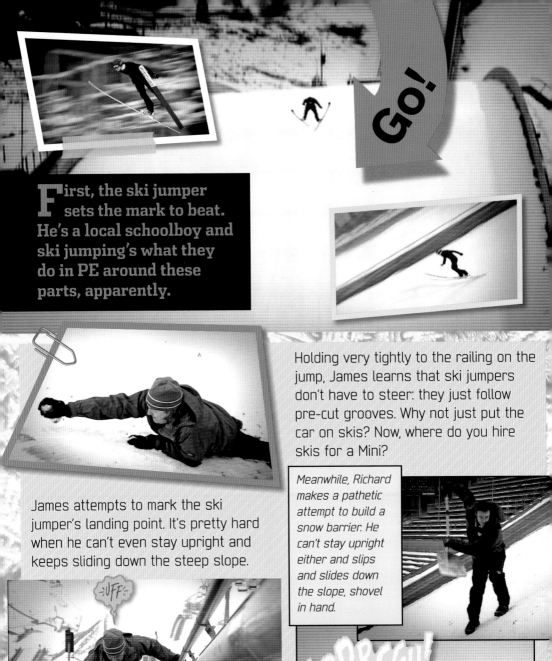

Go!

First, the ski jumper sets the mark to beat. He's a local schoolboy and ski jumping's what they do in PE around these parts, apparently.

Holding very tightly to the railing on the jump, James learns that ski jumpers don't have to steer: they just follow pre-cut grooves. Why not just put the car on skis? Now, where do you hire skis for a Mini?

James attempts to mark the ski jumper's landing point. It's pretty hard when he can't even stay upright and keeps sliding down the steep slope.

Meanwhile, Richard makes a pathetic attempt to build a snow barrier. He can't stay upright either and slips and slides down the slope, shovel in hand.

≈UFF≈

ARRRGGH!

Are these **really** going to give enough thrust?

This **is** rocket science.

Jeremy calls in the United Kingdom Rocketry Association to find out about the 'power!' The rocketeers reveal that by putting three rockets up the Mini's bottom, they can give it 1.5 tonnes of thrust – twice as much, weight for weight, as an F-15 jet fighter. Nevertheless, Jeremy is unimpressed by the size of the rockets. The rocketeers tell him they'll propel the Mini to 83mph at launch. The skier was doing 56mph.

The rocket men get to work on the rockets and the skis, while Jeremy has the tricky task of making the tea.

Jeremy and James meet up with Richard to inspect the barrier he's built. Jeremy has great joy in telling him he's built it next to the wrong jump. So Richard tries again with a snowplough and straw bales.

The Mini is towed up the ramp on its skis and prepared for launch. Richard is not confident. Too late to back out now!

This is **fairly** embarrassing.

5... 4... 3... 2... 1. **Ignition!** The rockets are fired. The Mini shoots down the slope, launches...

FFOOOM

And hits the landing point **nose-first!** Amazingly, it rights itself and continues with beautiful style to thump into the straw bales.
But did it beat the Norwegian?

FWAP

We were a **bit** short.

The winner

The might and engineering genius of Top Gear... was soundly beaten by a Norwegian schoolboy on this occasion. But the rocketeers are convinced they could win a rematch, so who knows...

Snowmobile Ski Jump

by The Stig

Glossary

4x4 – Short for four-wheel drive. Technically, a rear-wheel drive vehicle is sometimes called a 4x2. A unicycle, meanwhile, would be a 1x1. Are you seeing the pattern? With four-wheel drive vehicles, engine power goes to all four wheels, making it much less likely you'll get stuck in mud or spin off the road on an icy corner.

Aerodynamic – Used to describe a car that slips through the air easily. It's important because at motorway speeds, wind resistance soaks up about 60% of a car's power – even more if the dog's got its head out of the window.

Composite – Lightweight but strong material usually made by mixing glass or carbon fibres with resin (a sort of plastic). Composites are used in racing car bodies, crash helmets and loads of pointless things like gearknobs and key rings.

Controlled – Describes a car that's going round a corner sideways (see Drifting) where the driver seems to know what he's doing. Jeremy, James and Richard often claim to be 'controlled' shortly before they crash.

G-forces – Short for gravity forces. The feeling of being squashed against the side of a car that's going round a corner fast, or of being really heavy at the bottom of a rollercoaster dip. If you experience 2g, for instance, you feel twice as heavy.

Golden snow – Snow that someone has peed on. Avoid eating it.

Pirouette – A stationary spin. Used in dance, but very hard to do in a car, even when Jeremy's driving.

Puck – The thing ice hockey players hit when they're not hitting each other.

Drifting – This is where a car is sliding sideways but moving forwards at the same time. Rally drivers use drifting to bleed off speed while changing direction on loose surfaces, but on a racetrack, tyre-smoking drifts are actually not the fastest way to get round a corner. Great fun, though.

Floor it – To push the accelerator all the way down. Traditionally shouted by kids in the back seat when the family car is approaching a hump-back bridge.

Slalom – Weaving between a line of markers, passing one on the left, the next on the right etc.

SUV – Sports Utility Vehicle. Generally refers to a car that looks like a 4x4, might even be four-wheel drive, but is in fact pretty useless off-road.

Thrust – The force generated by a propeller, jet engine or rocket. It's measured in Newtons (N). If you weigh 45kg, you'd need to strap on a rocket with at least 442N of thrust to launch yourself into space. If you weigh 145kg... you need to think about dieting.

Tights – Mysterious form of leg coverings worn by women, ballet dancers and Richard Hammond when bobsleighing.

Traction control – Smart mechanical/electronic system designed to stop a car's wheels spinning. Often saves bad drivers from embarrassing themselves. Usually switched off by The Stig, who's hard to embarrass.

Trajectory – The curved path taken by an object thrown into the air.

Turbocharger – A pump that forces extra fuel and air into the engine at high revs, making it behave like a bigger engine and generating more power.

V8 – An engine with eight cylinders arranged in a 'V' formation, four cylinders per side.

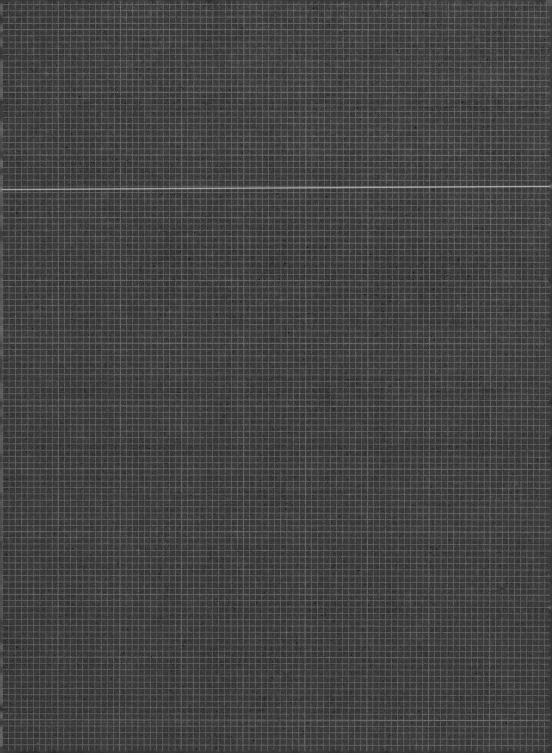